Summary of

Small Great Things:

A Novel by Jodi Picoult

By: Readtrepreneur Publishing

Proudly Brought to you by:

Legal & Disclaimer

Legal & Disclaimer

The information contained in this book is not designed to replace or take the place of any form of medicine or professional medical advice. The information in this book has been provided for educational and entertainment purposes only.

The information contained in this book has been compiled from sources deemed reliable, and it is accurate to the best of the Author's knowledge; however, the Author cannot guarantee its accuracy and validity and cannot be held liable for any errors or omissions. Changes are periodically made to this book. You must consult your doctor or get professional medical advice before using any of the suggested remedies, techniques, or information in this book. Images used in this book are not the same as of that of the actual book. This is a totally separate and different entity from that of the original book titled: "Small Great Things".

Upon using the information contained in this book, you agree to hold harmless the Author from and against any damages, costs, and expenses, including any legal fees potentially resulting from the application of any of the information provided by this guide. This disclaimer applies to any damages or injury caused by the use and application, whether directly or indirectly, of any advice or information presented, whether for breach of contract, tort, negligence, personal injury, criminal intent, or under any other cause of action.

You agree to accept all risks of using the information presented inside this book. You need to consult a professional medical practitioner in order to ensure you are both able and healthy enough to participate in this program.

Table of Contents

The Book at a Glance vi

Stage One: Early Labor 1

Ruth 1

Stage One: Active Labor 2

Ruth (1) 2

Turk (1) 4

Ruth (2) 6

Kennedy 10

Turk (2) 12

Ruth (3) 16

Stage One: Transition 18

Kennedy (1) 18

Turk (1) 21

Ruth (1) 23

Kennedy (2) 25

Ruth (2) 26

Kennedy (3) 27

Ruth (3) 28

Turk (2) 31

Kennedy (4) 32

Ruth (4) 34

Kennedy (5) 36

Stage Two: Pushing..**38**

    Ruth (1) 38

    Turk (1) 39

    Kennedy (1)... 40

    Ruth (2) 41

    Turk (2) 45

    Kennedy (2)... 46

    Ruth (3) 48

    Kennedy (3)... 49

    Ruth (4) 50

    Turk (3) 51

    Kennedy (4)... 52

    Ruth (5) 53

Stage Three: Afterbirth **54**

    Turk 54

Conclusion...**55**

BONUS – 3 Page Summary of Small Great Things.....**57**

A Small Favor **58**

The Book at a Glance

Stage One: Early Labor is told through Ruth's perspective. She talks about the experience she shared with her sister, mother, Mina and Christina Hallowell in bringing Louis into the world.

Stage One: Active Labor is told through different perspectives. It is still mostly from Ruth's perspective but Turk's perspective shows the other side of the situation. Kennedy is introduced in this part of the book to prepare her possible role in the future chapters.

Stage One: Transition is still told through the three perspectives. But it dwells more into the **reasons** why the characters are who they are. The description of how they became who they are is presented through their own point of view. There is Turk who had to deal with negative things from his personal lives that led him to become a White Supremacist. There is Ruth who became a nurse because of the hard work of her mother. Kennedy gets deeper into the situation that Ruth is in and would play a key role later.

The **death of Davis** is the main catalyst of the story and Ruth struggles against **the racism and prejudice** that she becomes even more sensitive about. She realizes how fragile the life she built really is.

Stage Two: Pushing is where the main conflict reaches its peak. Heavily invested into Ruth's case, Kennedy finds herself battling both the prejudice against her client and her client's prejudice against her. Meanwhile, Turk discovers valuable information that changes his life and his wife's, for the rest of their time together.

On the other hand, Ruth struggles to own up to her own **truths.** She learned to express who she is despite Kennedy's politically correct assumptions of what would win them the case. More truths are uncovered that leads to the resolution.

As Ruth's ordeal ends, Brittany's worst nightmare worsens. She finds out that her mother is African American. She can't come to grips with that truth and is **consumed by grief.**

Stage Three: Afterbirth is told through Turk's perspective. It is a few years after Ruth's case was resolved and he is a father once again. He reflects on how his life was after what happened and how he arrived at the current point in his life.

Small Great Things is a story of Ruth Jefferson who struggled all her life because of the prejudices she faced and the ones she tried to suppress. She has longed to belong to her own community but found it hard to deal with the discrimination of her own peers. She wanted to have a more peaceful life in the very community that considered her an outsider just because of the color of her skin. She wanted acceptance so she worked hard to **fit in.**

But ultimately, she realized that she was always going to feel like she was an outsider pressed against the glass, looking at the life of others. When she faced **her self-inflicted discrimination**, she freed herself from her own insecurities. She stood up for what she believed in and she spoke her mind towards the end of her trial. She didn't want to regret things as she did in the past. And thus, she was freed from her own doubts and misgivings.

The lives of Turk, Ruth, Francis, Brittany, and Kennedy showed how everything, good or bad, that happens to people, has an impact on their own lives and the lives of others. These characters were not intrinsically bad or good. They were simply presented as erring humans because of their own circumstances.

Turk grew up with a background that could lead a child astray. He found mentors in Raine and Francis who led him to a path that he would later regret. He was someone who hated a group of people simply because it was more **convenient to hate** them than face his own helplessness in certain areas of his own life.

Brittany believed what she wanted to believe and she was sure that she was someone who was superior to others because of the color of her skin. The revelation that she is the daughter of an African American woman was something that would shake her to the core.

She was a grieving mother, a child who believed that she was **abandoned** for a black man. But she loved fiercely and believed in their cause immensely. It was who she was and she wanted to make sure that her life partner was the same way. On the other hand, Francis was someone full of pride who didn't want to look bad in front of others and his daughter. However, the lie he kept didn't do anything good for Brittany. She hated her mother and never wanted to see her again but she did and it turned out that her mother would change her depression to desperation.

Kennedy made a road towards discovery in this book. She's always believed that she was one of the good guys and that she championed diversity. She thought of herself as someone who wouldn't be a racist. But as she handled Ruth's case, she discovered that in every **over-compensation** or every exaggerated way of showing compassion lays a kind of **passive racism**.

The theme of Small Great Things isn't just racism but <u>love</u> despite it all. The strength of a mother's love is seen in the perspectives of Ruth, Kennedy, and their own mothers. The grief brought on by the love of a parent, how it can make him blind to everything else, is seen in the Bauers' perspective. The value of how families work together to choose a better life is seen in the families of the Jeffersons, Hallowells and the Bauers.

What can be changed and what kind of life one can lead after a devastating tragedy such as the death of a loved one, is shown at the end of the book. Hate once filled Turk's life but he made it his life mission to show love and understanding rather than hate and division. He found that hate could still be an **inspiration** for a whole different reason.

Stage One: Early Labor

Ruth

Ruth goes to the house of her mother's boss. Mina Hallowell is pregnant and needs her mother's help. Christina is Miss Mina's daughter. Ruth's sister, Rachel wanted to play with her but they ended up playing doctor when they assisted their mother in delivering the son of Mina and Sam Hallowell. Ruth's mom was the one who delivered the baby but the rest of the children helped.

Ruth would later lament that it had fiercely different effects on the three of them. Christina opted for surrogacy. Rachel ended up having many children. Ruth became a nurse that assisted in births.

She thought that babies were **miracles** at that time. And she wanted to experience that miracle every time.

She would later have one of her own and her life would never be the same.

Stage One: Active Labor

Ruth (1)

Ruth believes that all babies are beautiful. She was having a difficult day in the birthing room that day. A faceless baby was born and it was going to die soon. It was so horrendous that a student nurse screamed. But without batting an eyelash, she asked the newbie nurse to leave the operating room and did the cleaning herself.

When the doctor told the parents that their child had birth defects and may not survive the day, the mother and the father had different reactions. The mother named their son as soon as she held him in her arms. The father, unable to accept, refused to hold the baby.

However, Ruth insisted that he give all the love stored up for a whole lifetime in the very little time that they had. She knew that it was the best way for the parents to cope with the loss of their child. They would have many questions as to why it happened but denying that the baby ever existed would have broken their family apart even faster.

When the father realized that it was his baby after all, he sobbed next to his wife. The baby died peacefully, but Ruth made sure to let the parents have a keepsake. She made casts of the hand and foot of Ian Michael Barnes for his mom and dad to remember their beautiful baby.

After finishing her task with Ian, she went to visit Jessie who was worried about how she looked after giving birth. She has never been around her husband without her full-on face. Ruth understood that perfectly and so she slipped into her room and helped Jessie fix her face and hair. An affinity between women showed that they are all worried that things would change between their husband and them once they have given birth.

At the nurse's station, they were talking about Corrine, the perennial latecomer. Ruth was talking to Marie while they wait. When Corrine arrived, they were assigned their new patients. Ruth got Brittany Bauer's file from Lucille. The latter warns her to look out for the dad.

She was attending to Baby Davis, but wondered why the father was looking at her a bit oddly. She was asked to stay away from Baby Davis when she mentioned a murmur in his heart. Turk, the father, is White Supremacist. Ruth was not doing anything wrong, but because of the **color of her skin**, Turk didn't want her attending to his son.

Turk (1)

Turk became a **White Supremacist** when his brother was killed in a car accident where a black man was driving the other car that hit him. The man was eventually acquitted and that started Turk's hatred and **victim mentality**. His family was never the same again after that. His father left and his mother was too devastated to take care of him properly. He later came to live with his grandfather who had a harsh way of raising him.

His grandfather constantly tried to teach him how to let go of his rage. He learned to bring out the negative emotions he had with his fists. But he was still a kid who had abandonment issues regardless of how old he was. There was a time when Turk's grandfather left him near Canada and he had to track his grandfather without much on him. He used his instincts to find his grandfather but instead of congratulating him, the old man just expected him to be grateful that he learned that from him.

Things were starting to get better for him when he got involved in an organization through a man named Raine, who worked in his father's bar. Turk got exposed to the readings first and found the ideals interesting. When he finally attended an event, he saw Brit's father speak there. All these events led him to Brit, who became his wife, the mother of his son, Davis. He was careful around her because she was a woman. But he later found out that she was, in fact, braver than he was.

But his initiation to organization came at a steep prize. He had to turn his back on his father completely. On a wilding with the North American Death Squad, he found out that his father was gay, the reason he left his mother.

He didn't want to be like his father.

He wanted to give his son a more traditional name but his wife put her foot down and refused to name their son after a superhero demigod.

So, when he was presented with the current situation where Ruth, someone like the people that both he and Brittany hated were talking to them about their precious son, he lost it.

He asked Ruth to bring her supervisor, Marie, and demanded that Ruth be **relieved of her duty** of taking care of his son. He showed his tattoo to make a point. Marie understood immediately.

Ruth (2)

Ruth was upset for various reasons. For one, it rarely happened. Second, the reason was the blatant implication of the post-it on Davis Bauer's chart. She was the only **African American nurse** in the hospital, so she considered this directive as a **personal attack.**

This wasn't the first time that she was asked not to touch a baby. There was a Muslim father who adamantly said that he was the first person to touch and talk to his child regardless of what happens to the birthing. She later found out that his religion led him to say a prayer to his child. It was a sharp contrast from Turk's reasons.

Ruth was upset and talked to her co-worker Corinne about it. But she realized that for people who were not in her situation, it was quite difficult for them to **empathize**.

She recalled how all her life, she was the odd girl out. It wasn't just because she was smart and that her mother insisted that she got bused to a better school. It wasn't that she didn't want to sound too black when she was in Cornell. It was that she always tried to be someone who could **blend in** and she ended up **compromising** a lot of things.

Growing up she seemed like the luckier sister simply because she was a bit fairer than her sister. This drove her sister to **embrace her ethnicity** to the extreme. Rachel changed her name and made sure to point out that Ruth was being too lax with identifying to who she really was. But as belongingness in the community was valuable to

Adisa – Rachel's new and more ethnic name – so was belongingness to Ruth, but in the world that her sister didn't even want to try to be in.

Gifted with a smart son, she decided to send him to a school where he could become more nurtured than ostracized. She also decided that it would be better for her son's future to live in the right address. One day she realized that there are things that would never change. Edison was upset that his close friend told him that he wouldn't be acceptable as a date for his sister. It was okay that they were friends but dating his sister was something his friend's parents would never allow.

She realized that they were still faced with the **limitations of people's perception** of them based on the color of their skin. She was getting pushed aside despite her twenty years of hard work and training. Her Merit Scholar son was not even a viable option because of how he looked like.

Ruth and Adisa might be different from each other or didn't look much alike since one was less dark than the other. But their difference doesn't stop one from seeking the other when it comes to needs for comfort. Adisa can be opinionated and passionate about her disposition against Ruth's assimilation into the White community but they still got each other's backs. Adisa pointed out that Ruth shouldn't expect that she would be treated equally or understood by the people around her since they never had to deal with what the two of them had to deal with. But Ruth's sister was not without her own tint of racism so Ruth called her out for it.

Despite having a hard time dealing with the Bauers, Ruth still went into an unscheduled shift. She still had looming thoughts about the heart murmur but she could only hope that someone already asked the doctor to check on the baby.

George and Eliza were the expectant parents this time. And Ruth couldn't help but wonder about George and if he would turn out to be just like Turk. But she was confronted with a different issue. Eliza mentioned that she was a rape victim and didn't know for sure if the baby was her husband's. It turned out the baby had George's blue eyes, nose, and cleft chin. Their daughter was a mini-George and all was well.

Ruth's day was packed. She was only able to see Corrine and Dr. Atkins when they were on their way to do Davis' circumcision. She made an off-hand remark that they should sterilize the baby after the procedure.

Ruth faced a dilemma when Corrine had to attend to another patient. The latter asked Ruth to watch Davis Bauer. It would have been okay, but the baby suddenly stopped breathing when she was left with the baby. She knew that she was not supposed to do anything to him because of the parents' request, but since the baby in a clear **emergency**, she decided to try to resuscitate him. It didn't work and she was taking a few seconds to think of what to do next when Marie

8

came in. She was **scared** that she would get into trouble for trying to help the baby so she said that she was not doing anything as per her instructions.

The head nurse asked her to call the code. Corrine, Dr. Atkins, Marie, and Ruth proceeded to try to revive the baby. She was the one doing compressions since they were short-handed. Unfortunately, it was too late, the **baby was dead**.

Turk and Brittany had come in during the revival. They were devastated. The couple tried to ask them to try again and not declare the time of death.

Afterwards, Marie talked to Ruth. She was curious as to why Ruth stood next to the baby without doing anything. As someone as well-trained as Ruth, it would not be normal behavior. Ruth still didn't tell anyone that she tried to help the baby before anyone else arrived.

Kennedy

Kennedy McQuarrie is a public defendant married to Micah, a doctor. They have a four-year-old daughter, named Violet.

Kennedy started her day with Violet using cuss words to get her way. It didn't get any better when she went to a prison to negotiate about wearing bras with underwire. She had to discuss the prison's dress code against bras while the other lawyer she was with said the rule against sandals was just as ridiculous. The warden relented eventually and said they would review their policies.

Kennedy talked about how if she hadn't met her husband, Micah, she would probably have a completely different life. She would not have thought of becoming a public defendant. Besides, she wouldn't be able to afford it financially. Micah was earning enough for their family, allowing her to do the work she does.

Her upbringing made her life with Micah both interesting and challenging. Her mother is a typical Southern belle. She would insert snippets of socially unacceptable ideas but Kennedy finds her love and support invaluable. Her mom has their best interest at heart but they hardly got along.

As an example, Kennedy's mom called for her so that she can get an appointment to use the spa treatment that her mom bought for her birthday. Kennedy was so uncomfortable that even the attendant pointed it out.

Having a kid means that she can't always have time with her husband. But they would try to have date nights. So, when her mom can't take care of Violet, she would have to make-do. And that was the case this time too. She had to bring Violet to the Indian restaurant and Micah couldn't do anything about that. They had a typical family dinner with Violet spouting some silly things that made Kennedy feel a bit embarrassed.

Turk (2)

The mood of Kennedy's family was the exact opposite of the Bauer's. Turk was back in the duplex owned by his father-in-law, Francis Mitchum, the legendary leader of the White Alliance Army.

Brittany was not herself when she got back to their home. Turk couldn't believe how horrible it made him feel to see his wife so broken because of what happened.

Turk was wondering – through his own **grief and anger** – what he should do with the nursery he helped put together for their son. He was sleep-deprived with a wife sleeping and calm only because she was sedated. He mulled over whether to just destroy everything with his bare hands.

He told Francis that he would just donate the items in the nursery to the Aryan Women's League. He didn't want any reminders of what happened. When he has another baby with Brittany, he didn't want her to remember the pain.

Thinking about the past glory of the movement that was now reduced to internet- supported political groups, Turk felt compelled to do something **drastic**. Thus, he went into the bathroom and shaved off his hair. The big black swastika tattoo that he had was a clear sign of his past. Francis called him out since they were supposed to be undercover but Francis understood that Turk was too angry to put into words. Turk was getting ready to go **berserk** again and he was going to **war** for Davis.

He went to the hospital dressed up in a suit, with his tattoos out for all to see. Brittany didn't want to go back to the hospital but it was important that they did. He helped her get ready but by the time they were in the hospital she was almost catatonic. He talked to the hospital lawyer and she convinced him that he shouldn't sue the hospital but Ruth Jefferson.

He went to the police to file a report and started off an investigation regarding what happened to his son. He met Sergeant Douglas there and Turk insisted that Ruth killed his son to get back at him and his wife for firing her because they were uncomfortable with having her around Davis.

He got a call from Sergeant Douglas regarding the medical report that could corroborate Turk's claim. The policeman said he would call the district attorney regarding the case. Turk was determined that if he could not bring back Davis, he would get **justice** for all of them.

When Brittany and Turk buried their son, Turk felt like he was slowly losing his wife, too. But there was a moment when she reached for his hand. He felt **hopeful** that they would survive this tragedy together.

Brittany and Turk went into the police station days after the funeral and got asked many questions on what happened. Brittany was upset about the way the police referred to Davis as an "it". Turk went out, feeling the need to bash someone's head in, black or not.

The tragedy was also a contrast to the way that Brittany and Turk first met.

A flashback of how Turk transitioned from being just a death squad member to a leader started off when he moved to Hartford. He had started taking classes at the community college there when he met Yorkey, a skater who seemed dissatisfied with the blacks too. He tried to do what Raine did for him and made Yorkey promise to give up drugs. Turk didn't want addicts in his crew because he believed that they were snitches.

He started recruiting people based only on the premise that they are **white and oppressed**. He sought out people who were bullied and entitled but were not given any chance to get what they wanted. He took care of them and made them believe that they had people who were protecting them. He got them to listen to music, read up on supremacist dogma and more importantly, give up whatever substance they were smoking or using.

That was how he made the Hartford division of NADS. They earned money selling guns to blacks. It played to their goal of getting rid of all the blacks in the vicinity.

Turk is an extremely loyal person. So, when they were in trouble for possession, he took the heat off Yorkey by not telling the police that the meth in his glove compartment was not his.

When he went to prison he was surrounded by black gangs. He kept to himself to survive the place long enough to serve his time. He ended up reading the Bible all the time. He even joined the jail's Bible study group. He met Twinkie there. Somehow, they got along despite Turk's deep disregard for black people. But he made an offhand remark once that lead Twinkie to stop associating with him. His **racist slur** caused him a friend in prison.

When he got out he went to found Yorkey, who by then, had aligned himself a group of bikers called Pagan. Turk's past berserker story got a new chapter then when he defeated twelve Pagan bikers with his speed and strength.

The story of his victory reached Francis Mitchum of the White Alliance Army. That was an eventful day not only because he met Francis again after having only seen him speak at a convention, but it was also the day he met Brittany.

Francis was considering the possibility of taking the skinheads' agenda into the new millennium. He handpicked Turk to be the guy who would help him do that. With the incentive that he could see Brittany often, Turk agreed immediately.

Ruth (3)

For Ruth, life went on as a nurse. She would think about Davis from time to time but in the hectic life she led in the hospital, it was not that often. Until she got a call from Carla Luongo, the hospital lawyer, she was busy trying to move past that experience.

Carla told Ruth that she talked to everyone present at the incident. There was an underlying threat in the way that Carla spoke to Ruth. That is, if Ruth would be suing the hospital, her career as a nurse would be over.

But despite the unpleasant conversation she had with Carla, Ruth went back to work. She was introduced to Virginia, a student nurse. When she went to assist a patient, she was mistaken for the assistant than the actual nurse in charge. Ruth felt that she was experiencing discrimination more clearly after the sensitive talk she had with the hospital lawyer.

Whenever Ruth felt like she needed the most comfort, she didn't go to Adisa. She would go to her mother, who still worked for Mina Hallowell. Her mother would insist that Mina still needs her, but truth is, she was too old to do much housework.

Ruth talked to her mom and reminisced on how her mother used to take them to the Hallowell's to work on Saturdays. She realized that the time she spent doing different chores there helped her in her work as a nurse. However, there were times in the past when she encountered Mr. Hallowell, who talked about how colored television was not that common and he had to say his famous line on NBC. That encounter gave her a nightmare the succeeding night.

She didn't want to worry her mother about the talk she had with the lawyer or the incident with the Bauers. However, she did mention what happened with the patient assuming that Virginia was the one in charge and not her. Her mother said that it was possible that the patient didn't mean anything by it but Ruth still felt bad.

Mina and Christina came in and Ruth was greeted by old friends. Christina ushered her to a room where she saw a miniature boat and realized that there was a miniature slave there, too. Ruth continues to see **reminders of her situation**.

Christina was oblivious to that and she had her own story to tell. Her husband was going to run for office and she was reluctant about that. Ruth listened and reacted attentively.

When Lou came in to give them some cookies, Christina thanked Lou for being part of their family. Ruth couldn't help but think that family members don't get a paycheck.

Stage One: Transition

Kennedy (1)

Kennedy's day was more typical than Ruth's. She met the new kid in their office, Howard. He was an African American newbie lawyer. Kennedy tried to be friendly but ended up having typical **misinformed assumptions about blacks**, in general, being poor. It turned out he is from Darien, an affluent part of the state.

She went to the New Haven Superior Court for the arraignment day. She helped a young man named Joseph get bail for possession with intent to sell. She didn't get him out of a hefty bail but his family could afford it.

She met Ruth shortly afterwards. The state lawyer, Odette, painted a dreadful picture regarding Ruth's case. The nurse was visibly upset about what had happened to her but Kennedy urged Ruth to trust her to speak on Ruth's behalf because the latter would just make things more difficult. However, she didn't have enough time to talk to Ruth so she asked the judge for time to talk to her for longer than ten seconds. The judge allowed it and they would set the bail at a second calling.

After doing her other arraignments, Kennedy talked to Ruth who was still upset. She asked basic questions she thought would help Ruth's case. Ruth talked to Kennedy about Turk and Brittany Bauer's request that led to a lot of the things that happened later. Kennedy didn't know at that time that Ruth was hiding the fact that she did try to help the baby. So, all Kennedy knew was that the parents of Davis were white supremacists who didn't like Ruth and that led her not try to touch Davis when the baby needed it. This resulted in the baby dying.

When Kennedy went back out to the courtroom, she felt like she could see things and people in a different way. She became more **aware** of the smaller signs of people's **biases**. If they wore something different, or if they had tattoos, or if they have unusual hairstyles. She finally had an idea of their affiliations.

She got to talk to Edison and assured him that she would do her best. She did try. The judge set the bail at one hundred thousand dollars with the help of posting the Jefferson's house. She assured Ruth that she would get out in a couple of days.

Kennedy felt for the Jeffersons but she knew that they would never give her a murder case. So, she left her contact information with Edison before telling him the possibility of her not getting his mother's case.

When Kennedy got home, Ruth's case still haunted her. Her mother was there taking care of Violet. They talked about how Violet wanted to be Tiana and minor discussions about race set the tone for the conversation. Kennedy's mom mentioned that she had a black nanny who was like family. Kennedy shares Ruth's thoughts that family doesn't get a paycheck. With her conversation with Micah, she mentioned about how some of the bad guys in Lion King are ethnic and spoke in black or Latino slang. Her husband told her she is over thinking it. That was then that she realized that she would do whatever she could to get Ruth's case and set her free.

Turk (1)

Turk went into the office of Roarke Matthews to get legal advice. He didn't expect to hear the lawyer's advice not to sue Ruth in a civil case until the criminal case was done. The lawyer made it quite clear that things would be delayed and that unless Ruth was rich and had money to pay Turk for settlement for the civil case, it would be pointless. This was when Turk's rash act of suing Ruth for murder got in the way of his wish to prevent Ruth from being a nurse.

In this chapter, more of Turk and Francis' past is revealed. Francis wanted Turk to help him change the terrain of their battles. Turk's main motivation, however, wasn't just spreading the ideals of their movement, but Brittany, as well. He was hesitant to ask her out but was relieved when Brittany made the first move. She convinced him to take her to one of his wildings.

He discovered more about Brittany and her mother while they were waiting out to attack.

Despite a recollection of how he met Brittany, the memories of his son still haunted Turk. His father-in-law let him grieve but drew the line after two weeks. He told Turk to **get even** and Turk did that using LONEWOLF.org – the website that he created with Francis. He wrote about what happened to his son and unmasked himself in the website. He became a person, not just an administrator.

Readership spiked and comforting and supportive comments flooded in. Turk felt like he has started yet another crusade.

When he went into the courtroom on the morning of the arraignment, some twenty Lonewolf followers were there to show their support. But when he couldn't handle his anger, he was sent out. This incident didn't stop him. He was more than **determined to win** this war against the black woman who killed his son.

He decided that it would better to catch them with honey than vinegar and asked his father-in-law to get Brittany out of the house. They needed to show that they were being discriminated and not the other way around. He spoke to the reporters about who he was and complained about how he was being treated. He got their attention.

But the attention he wanted to get was Ruth's, so he made sure that he was the last person she saw before she was bused off to prison.

With Turk and Francis' effort, LONEWOLF was launched and they put the information that was relevant to the people sympathetic to their cause. And instead of doing random wildings, they did vandalism that would cause articles to be written about the ideals they were fighting for.

The Brittany he married then was now a shadow of the Brittany of today. But after he got himself on TV speaking about the injustice that they experienced a part of the old Brittany came back and was happy to see him fighting for their son.

22

Ruth (1)

While the Bauer's were celebrating the initial victory of sending her to prison, Ruth was desperate to get things rolling so she could get out as soon as possible. She talked to Kennedy about how long she had to wait.

Ruth encountered her first inmate in the holding cell. The reality of meeting Liza Lott in prison, asking her what she is in for didn't shake her hope that Kennedy would really get her out in a couple of days.

Ruth reminisced how her mother loved that fact that she was going to Yale Nursing School. Her mother had always believed what Martin Luther King Jr. believed, that one must do small things in a great manner. She told her mother about the great things about going there but conveniently shielded her mother from the **small yet obvious discrimination** she experienced while living as a student there.

She bought a travel mug that said, "Yale". It was her shield from the way that people treated her. She would continue to do the same thing but using different shields: buying a house in a white community, sending her son to a school where the population is mostly white, affluent people, and working in a hospital where she is the only African-American nurse. It was the only way she could say "I am one of you."

She met her inmate Wanda, who became instrumental in making her doubt herself and all that she has done. She later met the prison counselor and was briefed on the rules. She tried to ask about how she could get in touch with her son but was told that the process to let a minor visit would take ten days. She didn't want him to come if it took that long.

When Ruth was rudely awakened to leave the prison cell, she was still scared because of what happened the last time she was handcuffed. Turns out, she was officially out on bail, and Edison was there to be with her when she went out.

Kennedy (2)

Kennedy believed that there were two kinds of public prosecutors, the idealistic ones, and the realistic ones. So, when she dreamt of Ruth twice, she knew that it would bother her if she didn't get her case. She asked Howard to be her second chair.

She was anxious to meet Ruth again so she tried to practice how she would greet her new client, but Ruth had been released. She ended up visiting Ruth at home to discuss the details of the case. Kennedy tried to get on Ruth's side and **gain her trust** so that she could get all the relevant information she needed to win the case.

She tried to convince Ruth that the case isn't about her race but because of neglect of duty. Kennedy presented the idea to Ruth that her situation can get better and she might even end up getting a chance to sue the hospital for the treatment she got. However, she would only have that chance if she is acquitted.

She promised Ruth that she would do her best without playing the **race card**.

Ruth (2)

Prison deeply affected Ruth. She woke up in sweats and went on to try to calm herself by watching her son sleep.

She went to the public defender's office after carefully choosing her outfit. There, she met Kennedy again. She wondered why the female defender ended up with her case. The conversation was now taking place from Ruth's perspective. The seemingly innocent questions that Kennedy asked brought back flashbacks of how black people's issues got twisted and turned into white issues cloaked in the **guise of equality**. She didn't want to, but she realized that Kennedy knew what she was doing. The lawyer said that the payout she would get from suing the hospital would only come about if she didn't make it a race issue to get acquitted.

Kennedy (3)

Kennedy's mom watched Violet again. She was grateful about that until her daughter made an unusual comment. Kennedy was quick to ask her mother about what they watched. She was shocked to find out that her mom had watched Fox News while her daughter was supposedly sleeping. Kennedy couldn't do much to argue with her mother because her daughter was already asking her to read a story for her.

Ruth (3)

Adisa offered to buy Ruth lunch so they could talk and unwind. They saw a show on TV about a man called Wallace Mercy, an **activist pastor**. Ruth was appalled by her sister's suggestion that they should ask Wallace to help her. She didn't want to make a **media spectacle** out of her case.

She visited Christina next and the **sharp contrast** of the support that Adisa showed her happened in Christina's home. The latter wanted to know how she was but Ruth felt that her friend was giving her the boot. Ruth stormed off while Christina tried to give her some money to help somehow. Ruth left it behind and took her **remaining pride** with her.

However, she had to **give that pride up** when she went to get welfare. She never wanted to be on welfare but there was no choice. She managed to get financial aid but she decided that working suited her more.

She got a job as a crew member at McDonald's. Her son, Edison, came by with his classmates and was surprised to see his mother there. When they got home, Edison tried to convince her to stop working by giving her his savings. He mentioned that he couldn't bear being in school because of how people were treating him. His classmates were **teasing** him while his teachers were **being too nice**.

When Ruth got a visit from Wallace Mercy she was giddy at first. But when he started to talk to her about advocating for her cause, she became wary. Before he left, he showed her the support that was flowing her way through the viewers of his show. However, for now, she preferred to do things her way.

Ruth remembered that even back when her husband was around, there were instances when discrimination **tainted their happier moments**. Despite that, because they were happy and younger, she pushed it aside and **focused on her happiness**.

Each day presented challenges for her and she overcame them, one by one. Her experience in being under pressure helped her get through all of it. One day Kennedy went to the same McDonald's. Ruth asked Kennedy if there were any news about her case, but there wasn't any.

Ruth remembered pieces of her past like the time when Mr. Hallowell helped her get over her fear of school. She had stomachaches from the stress but she was in denial. He told her that he felt the same once before. It was when he got promoted and felt like he didn't deserve it. He said that the cure was to find the **confidence to believe** that one didn't get to where they were by accident or because of the help of others. He said that Ruth was in her school because of her talents and her immense effort.

The same feeling of **helplessness** crept into her when she was called in when Edison got into a fight. He said that it was because people were making fun of him and he couldn't bear it anymore. He was in the middle of getting grounded when Kennedy dropped by.

When they talked about the case, Kennedy kept insisting that race was not a good card to play. She tried to probe about the medical reason for Davis' death. She was trying to find a loophole to exploit. However, Ruth was getting even more **frustrated**. It was clear that things wouldn't have happened if she was not pulled off the patient just because of her skin color. Since Kennedy didn't seem to get it, Ruth turned to Wallace for help.

Turk (2)

Meanwhile, life at the Bauers was getting worse by the day. Francis usually invited people from the Movement every other Sunday afternoon. He knew they couldn't put it off forever. It had been three months since they lost Davis. Brittany found it all too taxing. When she saw Turk holding a baby, it put her on edge.

She later tried to get him to **act and not just post** about the things that happened to them. Turk didn't think Francis would go with it but Brittany insisted that action was better than posting. So, Turk reached out to the one person who started it all, Raine.

When he visited Raine however, he discovered that the man who helped him get into the Death Squad had turned his back on the movement. Turk was hurt and was compelled to end their friendship.

He visited the other leaders and they were all **unwilling to take the risk**. Their assimilation was so complete that they couldn't risk it. Brittany was disappointed but tried to give him comfort, too. This time, it was Turk who turned her away. He had too many thoughts going through his mind that he couldn't make love to her.

He **reminisced** how happy they were on their wedding day. Once again, he felt the cold sheets against his hands when he reached for her in the middle of the night.

Kennedy (4)

While Brittany and Turk were spending time apart, Micah and Kennedy were talking about Ruth and her situation. Kennedy was convinced that Ruth hates her. She kept talking about how it was more rational not to take up race as a focal point in the case. But Micah didn't seem to agree with her.

Kennedy was furious to get a call from Reverend Wallace Mercy.

She rushed to Ruth's home to try to convince her that getting Wallace's help would hurt her case more than it could help it. She managed to convince Ruth that she can avoid all the **media fiasco** that would ensue once Wallace Mercy came onboard. She did this by telling Ruth that Kennedy would put Ruth on the stand to talk about what happened to her.

During the case, Kennedy noticed that some of **Ruth's ideals** might be rubbing off on her. She found that she was becoming more **sensitive** in the way people hide their racist remarks. She managed to get Jack DeNardi admit, in his own words, that Ruth's race was the reason she cannot be promoted.

Kennedy realized further when she asked Ruth to go shopping with her. She witnessed how she was not considered as a person of interest when it came to security checks but Ruth had gotten special attention on routine checks. When they were done shopping, Kenny finally understood what Ruth was trying to tell her.

Kennedy realized that even if for most things, they share a common space or preferences, the **differences** they have were **not just driven by choice**. There were environments wherein a woman of color would be a person who wasn't inherently considered as safe while Kennedy was not seen as any kind of threat.

When she found out that Judge Thunder was the judge for Ruth's case, she was wary. He hated media circus cases and with Wallace Mercy with Adisa outside the courthouse with his supporters singing, the chances of this being a regular case were already gone.

Ruth (4)

Meanwhile, Ruth was having another bad day. She almost had an altercation with a young woman who was rude to her and talked with a black accent. She avoided it only to be stressed out by the news from Kennedy that Wallace and Adisa put up a display at the courthouse to show support for her.

Ruth went to ask Adisa about it. Adisa thought it would help Ruth. The latter was distracted by the fact that her son was hanging out with Adisa's son. Tabari was not the kind of boy who Edison usually hung out with. Much like Ruth, Edison didn't grow up around the kind of slang and life in New Haven. But he was **changing** before her eyes because of all the things that were happening around them. She remembered how worried she was to have Edison and not know how to be a mother. Also, she **missed** how her mother reassured her that she would learn eventually.

She met up with Kennedy for her case often and she brought Edison with her sometimes. They had some interesting conversations about how slavery wasn't a solely black history and the contrast of how Violet asked her curious questions and shifted back to her other interests made the adults feel like the **young really did not have inherent prejudices**.

Ruth remembered when she was younger, Adisa's friends used to make fun of her and her sister wasn't too friendly with her either.

However, when Adisa's friends tried to hurt Ruth, Adisa didn't care if she lost her friends just to protect her only sister.

The bond of their family was more important when their mom died. Adisa told her that she called off the interview with Wallace. She didn't want it to drive a wedge between them.

After the funeral, Ruth met Kennedy's mother, Ava and she was given a revelation that even if her mother served the Hallowell's, her **service was not for naught**. Ava showed her a picture of her own caregiver and said that Ruth's mom's service was going to be **valued** by the people she loved for the rest of their lives.

Kennedy (5)

Although she got sick because of Micah, Kennedy was happy she married a doctor because he gave her an idea on how to get Ruth out of trouble. She asked him to get a neonatologist to look at the lab report he saw.

With that out of the way, she had to secure a jury that would be in Ruth's favor. So, she taught Howard how to investigate possible jurors.

Cross-checking references on social media and snooping around the neighborhood of the possible jurors helped them uncover some potential red flags. They found possible jurors likely to be **sympathetic to Ruth's plight.**

However, the main issue was Odette would veto any potential person they identified. She was also a woman of color but she didn't care about that. She only cared about her own work. Howard gave her hints that choosing some nice white people could be their hidden ace. Since Ruth was not as dark, there would be an **easy shift of prejudice**.

She received more good news when Micah told her that he got her a doctor who could explain the report to her, in a way that she can understand.

When the day to choose jurors came about, Kennedy knew that Ruth was even more nervous than she was. The process went on and Odette and Kennedy asked the jurors various questions before deliberating on who to keep and who to take out. Kennedy made sure that she got enough of the people she believed would help Ruth win the case than Odette would allow her to get away with.

Kennedy got the people she wanted with a couple of changes but she was satisfied with the jury. She went on to get more information about the lab report from Ivan, Micah's neonatologist friend. She discovered a **vital defense card**; Davis had MCADD and that the fasting that he went through caused him to have low blood sugar which caused his heart to fail.

However, Ivan was not sure if the baby could have been saved. This might help their case by **creating doubt**. If the test was done on a Monday, they would have been able to get the results faster. They wouldn't have put a baby on fasting if he had MCADD. Davis Bauer would still be alive if his screening sample wasn't sent out on a Friday.

Stage Two: Pushing

Ruth (1)

Ruth was getting ready to go to court and Edison was being difficult about it. She didn't know how to feel that she might be sent to prison at the end of the week but she was hopeful because Kennedy and her husband told her that there was an abnormality in Davis' lab report.

Although she saw the outpouring of support for her, she still had to keep her mind balanced and meet Kennedy where they previously discussed.

She fully trusted her lawyer. However, she still felt bad that she would be lying in court later if they asked her whether she helped Davis or not.

Turk (1)

Ruth was aiming to be discreet while Turk was not. Although Brittany followed the dress code their lawyer told her, Turk showed off his tattoos. He was going to make sure that people remembered their son and he was not going to **hide** who he was. They visited Davis' grave. The word LOVE was there just like the letters on his knuckles. He was going to carry his son with him and **avenge him at all cost**.

When he saw the group led by Wallace he was sickened but when he saw that the people from LONEWOLF.org had come out to support him and his family, he thanked them. They were willing to be outed just to help him seek justice for his son.

Kennedy (1)

While the two sides were pensive, Kennedy's morning was more frantic than ever. She rushed through her routine almost wearing two different shoes, if not for Violet's comment. She loved her supportive husband for trying to calm her down.

Her day with Ruth in court started with her reassuring the latter that all the things Ruth was worried she'd miss when she finally gets **thrown to prison** will not happen.

Ruth (2)

Ruth was nervously observing everything around her. She listened to Odette **downplay racism** that led to her being removed from caring for Davis Bauer and the emphasis was placed on what she would have done because of the negative feeling that it brought out in her. She felt like the jury was looking at her and judging her based on those words.

Kennedy's opening statement focused on how Ruth was in an impossible situation where she had to choose between whether to do something that would save Davis or defy her supervisor's order. She presented that fact that Davis had MCADD and that it was beyond even Ruth's ability to save him. She ended it on a note that pleaded that Ruth will not be blamed for something she could not have prevented, which was Davis Bauer's death.

As the trial progressed, more people came to testify for and against Ruth. Corinne talked about how Ruth said the infamous lines that led some people to believe that she was overly upset over being told that she couldn't take care of Davis anymore because she was black. Ruth was surprised that some of the things Corinne said were **exaggerated**. However, Kennedy cross-examined her well. Corinne basically admitted that she knew that Ruth could not help Davis even under an emergency because she was told not to but Corinne still left Davis in Ruth's care.

When Marie went up to the stand, Ruth remembered the moments when they were trying to save the baby.

Kennedy turned it around again when she pointed out that Marie didn't specify that in an event of an emergency and no other personnel was available that an African American medical personal could administer aid to the baby. So, there was no way for Ruth to know if she could have helped Davis.

Ruth was still mulling over her doubts during lunch, but she didn't want to show it to her son. When he asked her about what happened, she said it was even worse than what Marie said.

When it was Dr. Hager's turn to talk about what happened, Odette tried to make it sound like Ruth was trying to hurt the baby during the time she was doing compressions. However, Kennedy was quick to object and got Odette to stop with that line of questioning. Kennedy was on point when she asked Dr. Hager if everyone in the nursery at that time were trying to save Davis, including Ruth. To which the doctor answered a clear yes.

It was Dr. Atkins who repeated the joke she said about sterilizing the baby. During Kennedy's questioning, she successfully entered the lab report as evidence. Dr. Atkins mentioned about the screening done on babies and how one of the conditions that were tested for was

MCADD. When the doctor saw the lab report placed as evidence, the pediatrician said that Davis was **positive for MCADD.**

The first day was a win for them. When Ruth had a chance and was told by the prosecutor that she was just doing her job, Ruth couldn't help but snap back that she was lucky no one told her that she couldn't.

The second day was not looking good as Ruth was almost late. Luckily, Judge Thunder was late as well.

On that day, Sergeant Douglas was the first witness. Ruth knew that the Sergeant were spinning lies. However, Kennedy got the jury on their side when she pointed out that anyone would not be that cooperative if anyone barged into theirs home at three in the morning to arrest them.

Kennedy made a comment insinuating that the police tackled Edison to the ground because he was a young black man. Judge Thunder didn't like that statement and Kennedy told Ruth that that was the race card not used in court.

When the last witness, Dr. Bill Binnie was called in, he showed images of Davis to show how the body was checked. Brittany screamed around that time at Ruth and she was taken out of the courtroom. Turk followed her out. But Ruth knew that it caused the jury to **sympathize with Brittany and not her.**

When they came back after the recess, regardless of how Odette tried to play out that Ruth must have caused the death of Davis, Kennedy was able to make him say that because of his MCADD, Davis would have died even if Ruth tried to help him. Odette argued that they were just using the inconclusive screening results to help Ruth get out of the murder case.

When they got home Ruth and Edison talked about what he would have to do if Ruth went to jail. Ruth wanted her son to thrive and she would, of course, survive whatever happened.

Turk (2)

When they were ushered out of the courtroom, Turk was upset that their lawyer thought that Brittany was acting out but she assured him that he would need to be calm when he testified or everything would be ruined.

Odette asked him the questions regarding how he felt when he had Davis and about being a White Supremacist. Odette already told him that it was the other side's job to make them hate him. So, he needs to make sure to be clear of who he was - a father who just happened to be Pro-White.

When Kennedy questioned him, **Turk lost it**. He went after the lawyer. Odette told him that what he did cost them the case. She said that the prosecution rests. Turk wasn't willing to do that.

Kennedy (2)

Kennedy won the case for Ruth but Ruth still wanted to go to the stand and say her piece. They had essentially won the case so there was no need to do it. However, Ruth insisted but Kennedy was not sure it would be a good idea. Ruth told her that she did try to help Davis. Ruth demanded that she testify the next day. Kennedy knew then that they would lose this case if Ruth gets her way.

The next day, Kennedy was still trying to convince Ruth not to take the stand but she was stubborn about it. She told everyone what really happened when Kennedy was asking the questions very carefully. When it was Odette's turn, the aggressive questions **left Ruth's reliability and reputation in tatters**. Even if they could get the statements taken off the record, the jury still heard it and would be influenced by it.

Kennedy told Ruth that she did exactly what she was not supposed to do. Ruth admitted to her real emotions about being in the situation she was in. All her repressed emotions boiled to the surface. At the end of her tirade, Ruth fired Kennedy.

Because the judge dropped the murder charges, Ruth could not be charged twice. However, there was still an issue regarding her lying to the court.

Kennedy tried to reflect on what caused her to not see what Ruth saw. It struck her that the worlds they lived in were very different in a sense that people who might have been easy to talk to or deal with would have been wary because it was the norm. She concluded that what **she was avoiding was the exact thing that she would work in Ruth's favor.**

Ruth (3)

Ruth was worried about Edison not being home. When he came back he lied that he had been out running. Then the police arrived to **arrest** him for doing a **hate crime**. Ruth called Kennedy for help.

Kennedy (3)

Kennedy helped Edison out of the felony. He said that he only did it, to show people that not only Turk can paint the walls of the hospital with hate statements and symbols.

She instructed him to just follow her lead and she helped show the judge that it was an isolated case and that Edison was not going to do it again. It was more of an **impulsive act** due to his mother's situation.

When she was done with Edison's case, she went home and read files that sparked her interest. She then called Wallace Mercy to help her out.

Kennedy was surprised that Ruth still wanted her to represent her. She made a closing argument that had race as its theme. She presented the fact that because of Ruth's skin color, she was discriminated against and led to some unforeseen tragedies.

She also presented herself as a racist although she didn't know it at the beginning. But there was a kind of **racism that treats other people in a positive way**. Both kinds of racism cause people like Ruth to be in a difficult situation. She spoke about passive racism and it struck a chord with most of the people there.

Ruth (4)

Ruth was both surprised and relieved that Kennedy spoke about race in her closing statement. Although Kennedy was not positive about the result after Odette made her closing argument, Ruth was **happy to hear what Kennedy said**. She had wanted others to hear too.

Odette wasn't all that bad because she mentioned that the State was dropping the case against Edison and she complimented Kennedy for her closing. All they needed to do was to wait for the verdict.

When they went outside to meet up with the people who were there to support Ruth, Wallace Mercy came with a woman who approached Francis and Brittany. The woman was Adelle, Brittany's mother.

Brittany Bauer, daughter of the leader of the White Alliance Party, was half-black.

Turk (3)

Francis confessed that Adele was indeed Brittany's mother. He got jealous of someone and drove her away. Turk was worried about where Brittany could have gone. He looked for her in Davis' grave only to find her bloody from trying to take Adele's blood out of her.

Turk struggled with the fact that he still loved the woman who is the daughter of a black woman. That was when he knew that **his love for her would not change just because of what he found out.**

Kennedy (4)

The case ended in a **mistrial** because the jury was split. The judge dismissed the jury. Kennedy was surprised but happy when Judge Thunder used the escape hatch that she previously suggested. He granted the defense's motion and that meant that **Ruth was acquitted.**

Ruth (5)

Ruth couldn't believe that she was free to go. It took her some to realize it. She was ready to take on life again.

Stage Three: Afterbirth

Turk

Six years after the case, Turk was no longer married to Brittany. He was not a speaker who talked about his past. He was now a father to Carys, a beautiful little girl.

He met Ruth again, but now he had a different last name, having taken his wife, Deborah's last name, to start afresh. Ruth was Ruth Walker now, the owner of the same clinic he brought Carys. She helped Carys with her check-up.

All of them had come **full circle**.

Conclusion

Stage One: Early Labor talked about how the interactions started. It painted the initial emotions of the characters and later built up on how they created huge impacts on one another.

Stage One: Active Labor showed how the struggles they had in the past lead them to the lives they had when Davis' death occurred. There were still many things about each other that the others were not able to uncover.

Stage One: Transition slowly leads to the events that would later cause Ruth to come up with her own brave stance. As the tension built up, Kennedy would slowly be led to the realization that she was not as innocent in her dealings with other people of color.

Stage Two: Pushing was the tipping point. Turk and Ruth faced awful truths that they would have to own up to and they realized that love can conquer prejudices. Kennedy owned up to her own passive racism and delivers a closing remark that impresses everyone.

Stage Three: Afterbirth was a simple but beautiful closing. It was the first interaction between Ruth and Turk, six years after the events that changed both their lives. Their respective past may still be a part of them, but now, their past no longer hounds them. Turk has moved on from the tragedy that happened to his family. Ruth turned the events in her life as a stepping stone to improve her own life and that of her son's.

Small Great Things reminds us that when we think that we are not part of the problem, we are most likely wrong. Racism is just one aspect of discrimination. It is also discrimination if we cause good people to suffer and if we do nothing when see people suffer.

Discrimination shouldn't even be a thing in the modern world that we live in.

The fact that people are different and everyone should be proud of their individuality should be instilled in every person's mind.

The book teaches us that the things that we are afraid to say might be the truths the world needed to hear. It teaches us that if people begin to see beyond the physical aspects of each other, people can live peacefully, work together, and love one another, without prejudice and judgment.

Racism isn't something that can be defined by just one experience and the people who are experiencing it are not free from dishing it out. Being more understanding of each other and trying to create a world where our children would have the freedom to love whomever they want and be who they are must be the goal of every parent.

For everything starts from the home. It is the parents who will first teach their children how to treat any other individual.

The book tells its readers that family is important and what the children learn inside this smallest unit of society, will be what they will also bring out into the world. If children are taught about love, compassion, and understanding, then those are the things that they will bring out into the other people they will meet in their lifetime.

It starts with the home!

BONUS – 3 Page Summary of Small Great Things

You'll be receiving a downloadable PDF with all the key points of the book organized chapter-by-chapter.

Simply type the following link in a browser:

http://readtrepreneur.com/bonus/j8n3s-smallgreatthings

and enter your first name and email address in the web form. Your bonuses will be sent to you after confirming your email address. Enjoy!

A Small Favor

Hi, we hoped that you've enjoyed this summary read by Readtrepreneur Publishing. Could you help us by leaving us a honest review on Amazon?

You can easily do that by scrolling down after you've visited this link: http://readtrepreneur.com/bonus/j8n3s-smallgreatthings

before/after you claim the free pdf summary bonus!

Thank you so much and we hope that we've added tons of value into your life!

Wishing you the best,

Founder of Readtrepreneur Publishing,

Tommy King Wright

CPSIA information can be obtained
at www.ICGtesting.com
Printed in the USA
LVOW10s2245190917
549334LV00030BA/242/P